The Heraclidæ by Euripides

Euripides is rightly lauded as one of the great dramatists of all time. In his lifetime, he wrote over 90 plays and although only 18 have survived they reveal the scope and reach of his genius.

Euripides is identified with many theatrical innovations that have influenced drama all the way down to modern times, especially in the representation of traditional, mythical heroes as ordinary people in extraordinary circumstances.

As would be expected from a life lived 2,500 years ago, details of it are few and far between. Accounts of his life, written down the ages, do exist but whether much is reliable or surmised is open to debate.

Most accounts agree that he was born on Salamis Island around 480 BC, to mother Cleito and father Mnesarchus, a retailer who lived in a village near Athens. Upon the receipt of an oracle saying that his son was fated to win "crowns of victory", Mnesarchus insisted that the boy should train for a career in athletics.

However, what is clear is that athletics was not to be the way to win crowns of victory. Euripides had been lucky enough to have been born in the era as the other two masters of Greek Tragedy; Sophocles and Æschylus. It was in their footsteps that he was destined to follow.

His first play was performed some thirteen years after the first of Socrates plays and a mere three years after Æschylus had written his classic The Oristria.

Theatre was becoming a very important part of the Greek culture. The Dionysia, held annually, was the most important festival of theatre and second only to the fore-runner of the Olympic games, the Panathenia, held every four years, in appeal.

Euripides first competed in the City Dionysia, in 455 BC, one year after the death of Æschylus, and, incredibly, it was not until 441 BC that he won first prize. His final competition in Athens was in 408 BC. The Bacchae and Iphigenia in Aulis were performed after his death in 405 BC and first prize was awarded posthumously. Altogether his plays won first prize only five times.

Euripides was also a great lyric poet. In Medea, for example, he composed for his city, Athens, "the noblest of her songs of praise". His lyric skills however are not just confined to individual poems: "A play of Euripides is a musical whole....one song echoes motifs from the preceding song, while introducing new ones."

Much of his life and his whole career coincided with the struggle between Athens and Sparta for hegemony in Greece but he didn't live to see the final defeat of his city.

Euripides fell out of favour with his fellow Athenian citizens and retired to the court of Archelaus, king of Macedon, who treated him with consideration and affection.

At his death, in around 406BC, he was mourned by the king, who, refusing the request of the Athenians that his remains be carried back to the Greek city, buried him with much splendor within his own dominions. His tomb was placed at the confluence of two streams, near Arethusa in Macedonia, and a cenotaph was built to his memory on the road from Athens towards the Piraeus.

Index of Contents

THE PERSONS

IOLAUS.
COPREUS.*
CHORUS.
DEMOPHOON.
APOLLO.
MACARIA.*
SERVANT.
ALCMENA.
MESSENGER.
EURYSTHEUS.

*The names of Copreus and Macaria were wanting in the MSS., but have been supplied from the mythologists.

THE ARGUMENT

Iolaus, son of Iphiclus, and nephew of Hercules, whom he had joined in his expeditions during his youth, in his old age protected his sons. For the sons of Hercules having been driven out of every part of Greece by Eurystheus, he came with them to Athens; and, embracing the altars of the Gods, was safe, Demophoon being king of the city; and when Copreus, the herald of Eurystheus, wished to remove the suppliants, he prevented him. Upon this he departed, threatening war. Demophoon despised him; but hearing the oracles promise him victory if he sacrificed the most noble Athenian virgin to Ceres, he was grieved; not wishing to slay either his own daughter, or that of any citizen, for the sake of the suppliants. But Macaria, one of the daughters of Hercules, hearing of the prediction, willingly devoted herself. They honored her for her noble death, and, knowing that their enemies were at hand, went forth to battle. The play ends with their victory, and the capture of Eurystheus.

THE HERACLIDÆ

IOLAUS

This has long since been my established opinion, the just man is born for his neighbors; but he who has a mind bent upon gain is both useless to the city and disagreeable to deal with, but best for himself. And I know this, not having learned it by word of mouth; for I, through shame, and reverencing the ties of kindred, when it was in my power to dwell quietly in Argos, partook of more of Hercules' labors, while he was with us, than any one man besides: and now that he dwells in heaven, keeping these his children under my wings, I preserve them, I myself being in want of safety. For since their father was removed from the earth, first Eurystheus wished to kill me, but I escaped; and my country indeed is no more, but my life is saved, and I wander in exile, migrating from one city to another. For, in addition to my other ills, Eurystheus has chosen to insult me with this insult; sending heralds whenever on earth he learns we are settled, he demands us, and drives us out of the land; alleging the city of Argos, one not paltry either to be friends with or to make an enemy, and himself too prospering as he is; but they seeing my weak state, and that these too are little, and bereaved of their sire, respecting the more powerful, drive us from the land. And I am banished, together with the banished children, and fare ill together with those who fare ill, loathing to desert them, lest some may say thus, Behold, now that the children have no father, Iolaus, their kinsman born, defends them not. But being bereft of all Greece, coming to Marathon and the country under the same rule, we sit suppliants at the altars of the Gods, that they may assist us; for it is said that the two sons of Theseus inhabit the territory of this land, of the race of Pandion, having received it by lot, being near akin to these children; on which account we have come this way to the frontiers of illustrious Athens. And by two aged people is this flight led, I, indeed, being alarmed about these children; and the female race of her son Alcmena preserves within this temple, clasping it in her arms; for we are ashamed that virgins should mingle with the mob, and stand at the altars. But Hyllus and his brothers, who are older, are seeking where there is a strong-hold that we may inhabit, if we be thrust forth from this land by force. O children, children! hither; take hold of my garments; I see the herald of Eurystheus coming hither toward us, by whom we are pursued as wanderers, deprived of every land. O detested one, may you perish, and the man who sent you: how many evils indeed have you announced to the noble father of these children from that same mouth!

COPREUS
I suppose you think that this is a fine seat you are sitting in, and have come to a city which is an ally, thinking foolishly; for there is no one who will choose your useless power in preference to Eurydtheus. Depart; why toilest thou thus? You must rise up and go to Argos, where punishment by stoning awaits you.

IOLAUS
Not so, since the altar of the God will aid me, and the free land in which we tread.

COPREUS
Do you wish to cause me trouble with this band?

IOLAUS
Surely you will not drag me away, nor these children, seizing by force?

COPREUS
You shall know; but you are not a good prophet in this.

IOLAUS
This shall never happen, while I am alive.

COPREUS
Depart; but I will lead these away, even though you be unwilling, considering them, wherever they may be, to belong to Eurystheus.

IOLAUS

O ye who have dwelt in Athens a long time, defend us; for, being suppliants of Jove, the Presider over the Forum, we are treated with violence, and our garlands are profaned, both a reproach to the city, and an insult to the Gods.

CHORUS

Hollo! hollo! what is this noise near the altar? what calamity will it straightway portend?

IOLAUS

Behold me, a weak old man, thrown down on the plain; miserable that I am.

CHORUS

By whose hand do you fall this unhappy fall?

IOLAUS

This man, O strangers, dishonoring your Gods, drags me violently from the altar of Jupiter.

CHORUS

From what land, O old man, have you come hither to this people dwelling together in four cities? or, have you come hither from across the sea with marine oar, having quitted the Eubœan shore?

IOLAUS

O strangers, I am not accustomed to an islander's life, but we are come to your land from Mycenæ.

CHORUS

What name, O old man, did the Mycenæan people call you?

IOLAUS

Know that I am Iolaus, once the companion of Hercules; for this body is not unrenowned.

CHORUS

I know, having heard of it before; but say whose youthful children you are leading in your hand.

IOLAUS

These, O strangers, are the sons of Hercules, who are come as suppliants of you and the city.

CHORUS

What do ye seek? or, tell me, is it wanting to have speech of the city?

IOLAUS

Not to be given up, and not to go to Argos, being dragged from your Gods by force.

COPREUS

But this will not be sufficient for your masters, who, having power over you, find you here.

CHORUS

It is right, O stranger, to reverence the suppliants of the Gods, and not for you to leave by violent hands the habitations of the deities, for venerable Justice will not suffer this.

COPREUS

Send now Eurystheus's subjects out of this land, and I will not use this hand violently.

CHORUS

It is impious for a state to reject the suppliant prayer of strangers.

COPREUS

But it is good to have one's foot out of trouble, being possessed of the better counsel.

CHORUS

You should then have dared this, having spoken to the king of this land, but you should not drag strangers away from the Gods by force, if you respect a free land.

COPREUS

But who is king of this country and city?

CHORUS

Demophoon, the son of Theseus, of a noble father.

COPREUS

With him, then, the contest of this argument had best be; all else is spoken in vain.

CHORUS

And indeed hither he comes in haste, and Acamas, his brother, to hear these words.

DEMOPHOON

Since you, being an old man, have anticipated us, who are younger, in running to this hearth of Jove, say what hap collects this multitude here.

CHORUS

These sons of Hercules sit here as suppliants, having crowned the altar, as you see. O king, and Iolaus, the faithful companion of their father.

DEMOPHOON

Why then did this chance occasion clamors?

CHORUS

This man caused the noise, seeking to lead him by force from this hearth; and he tripped up the legs of the old man, so that I shed the tear for pity.

DEMOPHOON

And indeed he has a Grecian robe and style of dress; but these are the doings of a barbarian hand; it is for you then to tell me, and not to delay, leaving the confines of what land you are come hither.

COPREUS

I am an Argive; for this you wish to learn: and I am willing to say why, and from whom, I am come. Eurystheus, the king of Mycenæ, sends me hither to lead away these men; and I have come, O stranger, having many just things at once to do and to say; for I being an Argive myself, lead away Argives, having them as fugitives from my country condemned to die by the laws there; and we have the right, managing our city ourselves by ourselves, to fix our own punishments: but they having come to the hearths of many others also, there also we have taken our stand on these same arguments, and no one has dared to bring evils upon himself. But either perceiving some folly in you, they have come hither, or in perplexity running the risk, whether it shall be or not. For surely they do not think that you alone are mad, in so great a portion of Greece as they have been over, so as to commiserate their foolish distresses. Come, compare the two; admitting them into your land, and suffering us to lead them away, what will you gain? Such things as these you may gain from us; you may add to this city the whole power of Argos, and all the might of Eurystheus; but if looking to the words and pitiable condition of these men, you are softened by them, the matter comes to the contest of the spear; for think not that we will give up this contest without steel. What then will you say? deprived of what lands, making war with the Tirynthians and Argives, and repelling them, with what allies, and on whose behalf will you bury the dead that fall? Surely you will obtain an evil report among the citizens, if, for the sake of an old man, a mere tomb, one who is nothing, as one may say, and of these children, you will put your foot into a mess; you will say, at best, that you shall find, at least, hope; and this too is at present much wanting; for these who are armed would fight but ill with Argives if they were grown up, if this encourages your mind, and there is much time in the mean while in which ye may be destroyed; but be persuaded by me, giving nothing, but permitting me to lead away my own, gain Mycenæ. And do not (as you are wont to do) suffer this, when it is in your power to choose the better friends, choose the worse.

CHORUS
Who can decide what is right, or understand an argument, till he has clearly heard the statement of both?

IOLAUS
O king, this exists in thy city; I am permitted in turn to speak and to hear, and no one will reject me before that, as in other places; but with this man we have nothing to do; for since nothing of Argos is any longer ours, (it having been decreed by a vote,) but we are exiled our country, how can this man justly lead us away as Mycenæans, whom they have driven from the land? for we are strangers; or else you decide that whoever is banished Argos is banished the boundaries of the Greeks. Surely not from Athens; they will not, for fear of the Argives, drive out the children of Hercules from their land; for it is not Trachis, nor the Achæan city, from whence you, not by justice, but bragging about Argos; just as you now speak, drove these men, sitting at the altars as suppliants; for if this shall be, and they ratify your words, I no longer know this Athens as free. But I know their disposition and nature; they will rather die; for among virtuous men, disgrace is considered before life. Enough of the city; for indeed it is an invidious thing to praise it too much; and often I know myself I have been oppressed at being overpraised: but I wish to say to you that it is necessary for you to save these men, since you are ruler over this land. Pittheus was son of Pelops and Æthra, daughter of Pittheus, and your father Theseus was born of her. And again I trace for you their descent: Hercules was son of Jupiter and Alcmena, and she was the child of the daughter of Pelops; so your father and theirs must be fellow-cousins. Thus you, O Demophoon, are related to them by birth; and, besides this connection, I will tell you for what you are bound to requite the children. For I say, I formerly, when shield-bearer to their father, sailed with Theseus after the belt, the cause of much slaughter, and from the murky recesses of hell did he bring forth your father. All Greece bears witness to this; for which things they beseech you to return a kindness, and that they may not be yielded up, nor be driven from this land, torn from your Gods by violence; for this would be disgraceful to you by yourself, and an evil to the city, that suppliant relations, wanderers—alas for the misery! look on them, look—should be dragged away by force. But I beseech you, and offer you suppliant garlands, by your hands and your chin, do not dishonor the children of Hercules, having received them in your power; but be thou a relation to them, be a friend, father, brother, master; for all these things are better than for them to fall into the power of the Argives.

CHORUS
Hearing of these men's misfortunes, I pitied them, O king! and now particularly I have witnessed nobleness overcome by fortune; for these men, being sons of a noble father, are undeservedly unhappy.

DEMOPHOON

Three ways of misfortune urge me, O Iolaus, not to reject these suppliants. The greatest, Jupiter, at whose altars you sit, having this procession of youths with you; and my relationship to them, and because I am bound of old that they should fare well at my hands, in gratitude to their father; and the disgrace, which one ought exceedingly to regard. For if I permitted this altar to be violated by force by a strange man, I shall not seem to inhabit a free country. But I fear to betray my suppliants to the Argives; and this is nearly as bad as the noose. But I wish you had come with better fortune; but still, even now, fear not that any one shall drag you and these children by force from this altar. And do thou, going to Argos, both tell this to Eurystheus; and besides that, if he has any charge against these strangers, he shall meet with justice; but you shall never drag away these men.

COPREUS

Not if it be just, and I prevail in argument?

DEMOPHOON

And how can it be just to drag away a suppliant by force?

COPREUS

This, then, is not disgraceful to me, but an injury to you.

DEMOPHOON

To me indeed, if I allow you to drag them away.

COPREUS

But do you depart, and then will I drag them thence.

DEMOPHOON

You are stupid, thinking yourself wiser than a God.

COPREUS

Hither it seems the wicked should fly.

DEMOPHOON

The seat of the Gods is a common defense to all.

COPREUS

Perhaps this will not seem good to the Mycenæans.

DEMOPHOON

Am not I then master over those here?

COPREUS

Ay, but not to injure them, if you are wise.

DEMOPHOON

Are ye hurt, if I do not defile the Gods?

COPREUS

I do not wish you to have war with the Argives.

DEMOPHOON

I, too, am the same; but I will not let go of these men.

COPREUS

At all events, taking possession of my own, I shall lead them away.

DEMOPHOON

Then you will not easily depart back to Argos.

COPREUS

I shall soon see that by experience.

DEMOPHOON

You will touch them to your own injury, and that without delay.

CHORUS

For God's sake, venture not to strike a herald!

DEMOPHOON

I will not, if the herald at least will learn to be wise.

CHORUS

Depart thou; and do not you touch him, O king!

COPREUS

I go; for the struggle of a single hand is powerless. But I will come, bringing hither many a brazen spear of Argive war; and ten thousand shield-bearers await me, and Eurystheus, the king himself, as general. And he waits, expecting news from hence, on the extreme confines of Alcathus; and, having heard of your insolence, he will make himself too well known to you, and to the citizens, and to this land, and to the trees; for in vain should we have so much youth in Argos, if we did not chastise you.

DEMOPHOON

Destruction on you! for I do not fear your Argos. But you are not likely, insulting me, to drag these men away from hence by force; for I possess this land, not being subject to that of Argos, but free.

CHORUS

It is time to provide, before the army of the Argives approaches the borders. And very impetuous is the Mars of the Mycenæans, and on this account more than before; for it is the habit of all heralds to tower up what is twice as much. What do you not think he will say to his princes about what terrible things he has suffered, and how within a little he was losing his life.

IOLAUS

There is not, to this man's children, a more glorious honor than to be sprung from a good and valiant father, and to marry from a good family; but I will not praise him who, overcome by desire, has mingled with the vulgar, to leave his children a reproach instead of pleasure; for noble birth wards off misfortune better than low descent; for we, having fallen into the extremity of evils, find these men friends and relations, who alone, in so large a country as Greece, have stood forward on our behalf. Give, O children, give them your right hand; and do ye give yours to the children, and draw near to them. O children, we have come to experience of our friends; and if you ever have a return to your country, and again possess the homes and honors of your father, always consider them your saviors and friends, and never lift the hostile spear against the land, remembering these things; but consider it the dearest city of all. And they are worthy that you should revere them, who have chosen to have so great a country and the Pelasgic people as enemies instead of us, though seeing us to be beggared wanderers; but still they have not given us up, nor driven us from their land. But I, living and dying, when I do die, with much praise, my friend, will extol you when I am in company with Theseus; and telling this, I will delight him, saying how well you received and aided the children of Hercules; and, being noble, you preserve through Greece your ancestral glory; and being born of noble parents, you are nowise inferior to your father, with but few others; for among many you may find perhaps but one who is not inferior to his father.

CHORUS
This land is ever willing to aid in a just cause those in difficulty; therefore it has borne numberless toils for its friends, and now I see this contest at hand.

DEMOPHOON
Thou hast spoken well; and I boast, old man, that their disposition is such that the kindness will be remembered. And I will make an assembly of the citizens, and draw them up so as to receive the army of the Mycenæans with a large force. First, I will send spies toward it, that it may not fall upon me by surprise: for in Argos every warrior is eager to run to assistance. And having collected the soothsayers, I will sacrifice. And do you go to my palace with the children, leaving the hearth of Jove, for there are those who, even if I be from home, will take care of you; go then, old man, to my palace.

IOLAUS
I will not leave the altar; but we will sit here, as suppliants, waiting till the city is successful; and when you are well freed from this contest, we will go to thy palace. But we have Gods as allies not inferior to those of the Argives, O king; for Juno, the wife of Jove, is their champion, but Minerva ours; and I say that this also tends to success, to have the best Gods, for Pallas will not endure to be conquered.

CHORUS
If thou boastest greatly, others do not therefore care for thee the more, O stranger, coming from Argos; but with thy big words thou wilt not terrify my mind: may it not be so to the mighty Athens, with the beauteous dances. But both thou art foolish, the son of Sthenelus, king in Argos, who, coming to another city not less than Argos, being a stranger, seek by violence to lead away wanderers, suppliants of the Gods, and claiming the protection of my land, not yielding to our kings, nor saying any thing else that is just. How can this be thought well among the wise? Peace indeed pleases me; but, O foolish king, I tell thee, if thou comest to this city, thou wilt not thus obtain what thou thinkest for. You are not the only one who has a spear and a brazen shield; but, O lover of war, mayest thou not with the spear disturb my city dear to the Graces; but restrain thyself.

IOLAUS
O my son, why comest thou, bringing solicitude to my eyes? Hast thou any news of the enemy? Do they delay, or are they at hand I or what do you hear? for I fear the word of the herald will in no wise be false, for their leader will come, having been fortunate in previous affairs, I clearly know, and with no moderate pride, against Athens; but Jove is the chastiser of over-arrogant thoughts.

DEMOPHOON
The army of the Argives is coming, and Eurystheus the king. I have seen it myself; for it behooves a man who says he knows well the duty of a general not to reconnoitre the enemy by means of messengers. He has not then, as yet, let loose his army on these plains, but, sitting on a lofty crag, he reconnoitres (I should tell thee this as a conjecture) to see by which way he shall now lead his

expedition, and place it in a safe station in this land; and my preparations are already well arranged, and the city is in arms, and the victims stand ready for those Gods to whom they ought to be slain offered; and the city, by means of soothsayers, is preparing by sacrifices flight for the enemy and safety for the city. And having collected together all the bards who proclaim oracles, I have tested the ancient oracles, both public and concealed, which might save this land; and in their other counsels many things are different; but one opinion of all is conspicuously the same, they command me to sacrifice to the daughter of Ceres a damsel who is of a noble father. And I have indeed, as you see, such great good-will toward you, but I will neither slay my own child nor compel any other of my citizens to do so unwillingly; and who is so mad of his own accord, as to give out of his hands his dearest children? And now you may see bitter meetings; some saying that it is right to aid foreign suppliants, and some blaming my folly; and if I do this, a civil war is at once prepared. This, then, do you consider, and devise how both you yourselves may be saved and this land, and I be not brought into ill odor with the citizens; for I have not absolute sovereignty, as over barbarians; but if I do just things, I shall receive just things.

CHORUS

But does not the Goddess allow this city, although eager, to aid strangers?

IOLAUS

O children, we are like sailors, who, fleeing from the fierce rage of the storm, have come close to land, and then, again, by gales from the land, have been driven again out to sea; thus also shall we be driven from this land, being already on shore, as if saved. Alas! why, O wretched hope, did you then delight me, not being about to perfect my joy? For his thoughts, in truth, are to be pardoned if he is not willing to slay the children of his citizens; and I acquiesce in their conduct here, if the Gods decree that I shall fare thus. My gratitude to you shall never perish. O children, I know not what to do with you: whither shall we turn? for who of the Gods has been uncrowned by us? and what bulwark of land have we not approached!? We shall perish, my children, we shall be given up; and for myself I care nothing if it behooves me to die, except that, dying, I shall gratify my enemies; but I weep for and pity you, O children, and Alcmena, the aged mother of your father; O! unhappy art thou, because of thy long life; and miserable am I, having labored much in vain. It was our fate then, our fate, falling into the hands of an enemy, to leave life disgracefully and miserably. But do you know in what you may aid me? for all hope of their safety has not deserted me. Give me up to the Argives instead of them, O king, and so neither run any risk yourself, and let the children be saved for me; I must not love my own life, let it go; and above all, Eurystheus would like taking me, the ally of Hercules, to insult me; for he is a froward man; and the wise should pray to have enmity with a wise man, not with an ignorant disposition, for in that case one, even if unfortunate, may meet with much respect.

CHORUS

O old man, do not now blame the city, perhaps it might be a gain to us; but still it would be an evil reproach that we betrayed strangers,

DEMOPHOON

You have spoken things noble indeed, but impossible; the king does not lead his army hither wanting you; for what profit were it to Eurystheus for an old man to die? but he wishes to slay these children; for noble youths, who remember their fathers' injuries, springing up, are terrible to enemies; all which he must needs foresee; but if you know any other more seasonable counsel, prepare it, since I am perplexed and full of fear, having heard the oracle.

MACARIA

O strangers, do not impute boldness to me because of my advances, this I will beg first; for silence and modesty are best for a woman, and to remain quietly in-doors; but, having heard your lamentations, O Iolaus, I have come forth, not being commissioned to act as embassador for my race, but I am in some wise fit to do so; but chiefly do I care for these, my brothers: concerning myself I wish to ask whether, besides our former evils, any additional distress gnaws your mind?

IOLAUS
O daughter, it is not a new thing that I justly have to praise you most of the children of Hercules; but our house having appeared to us to progress well, has again changed to perplexity, for this man says, that the deliverers of oracles order us to sacrifice not a bull or a heifer, but a virgin, who is of a noble father, if we and this city would exist. About this then we are perplexed, for this man says he will neither slay his own children nor those of any one else; and to me he says, not plainly indeed, but somehow or other, unless I can devise any remedy for this, that we must find some other land, but he himself wishes to preserve this country.

MACARIA
On this condition can we then be saved?

IOLAUS
On this, being fortunate in other respects.

MACARIA
Fear not then any longer the hostile spear of the Argives; for I myself, old man, before I am commanded, am prepared to die, and to stand for slaughter; for what shall we say if the city thinks fit for our sakes to encounter a great danger, but we putting toils on others, avoid death when we can be saved? Not so, since this would be ridiculous for suppliants sitting at the shrines of the Gods to mourn, but being of such a sire as we are, to be seen to be cowards; how can this seem good! it were more noble, I think, (which may it never happen!) to fall into the hands of the enemy, this city being taken, and afterward, being born of a noble father, having suffered dreadful things, to see Hades none the less; but shall I wander about, driven from this land, and shall I not indeed be ashamed if any one says, "Why have ye come hither with your suppliant branches, yourselves being too fond of life! Depart from the land, for we will not aid cowards." But neither, indeed, if these die, and I myself am saved, have I any hope to fare well; for before now many have in this way betrayed their friends. For who would choose to have me, a solitary damsel, for his wife, or to raise children from me? therefore it is better to die than to have such an unworthy fate as this; and this may even be more seemly for some other, who is not illustrious as I. Lead me then where this body must needs die, and crown me and begin the rites, if you think fit, and conquer your enemies; for this life is ready for you, willing, and not unwilling; and I promise to die for these my brethren, and for myself; for not caring for life, I have found this most glorious thing to find, namely, to leave life gloriously.

CHORUS
Alas! alas! what shall I say, hearing this noble speech of the maiden who is willing to die on behalf of her brothers? Who can utter more noble words than these I who of men can do a greater deed?

IOLAUS
My child, your head comes from no other source, but thou, the seed of a divine mind, art sprung from Hercules. I am not ashamed at your words, but I am grieved for your fortune; but how it may be more justly done, I will say: we must call hither all her sisters, and then let her who draws the lot die for her family; but it is not right for thee to die without casting lots.

MACARIA

I will not die, obtaining the lot by chance, for then there are no thanks to me;—speak it not, old man; but if you accept me, and are willing to use me willing, I readily give up my life to them, but not, being compelled.

IOLAUS

Alas! this word of thine is again nobler than the former, and that other was most excellent; but you surpass daring by daring, and good words by good words. I do not bid you, nor do I forbid you, to die, my child; but you will benefit your brothers by dying.

MACARIA

Thou biddest wisely; fear not to partake of my pollution, but I shall die freely. But follow me, O old man; for I wish to die by your hand; and do you, being present, wrap my body in my garments, since I am going to the terror of sacrifice, because I am born of the father of whom I boast to be.

IOLAUS

I could not be present at your death.

MACARIA

At least, then, entreat of him that I may die, not by the hands of men, but of women.

CHORUS

It shall be so, O hapless virgin; since it were disgraceful to me too not to deck thee honorably on many accounts; both for your valiant spirit, and for justice' sake: but you are the most unhappy of all women that I have beheld with mine eyes; but, if thou wilt, depart, bespeaking a last address to these and to the old man.

MACARIA

Farewell, old man, farewell; and train up for me these children to be such as thyself, wise in all respects, nothing more, for they will suffice; and endeavor to save them, not being over-willing to die. We are your children; by your hands we were brought up, and behold see me yielding up my nuptial hour, dying for them. And ye, my company of brothers now present, may ye be happy, and may every thing be yours, for the sake of which my soul is sacrificed; and honor the old man, and the old woman in the house, Alcmena, the mother of my father, and these strangers. And if a release from troubles, and a return should ever be found for you through the Gods, remember to bury her who saves you, as is fitting; most honorably were just, for I was not wanting to you, but died for my race. This is my heir-loom instead of children and virginity, if indeed there be aught under the earth. May there indeed be nothing; for if we, mortals who die, are to have cares even there, I know not where one can turn, for to die is considered the greatest remedy for evils.

IOLAUS

But, O you, who mightily surpass all women in courage, know that, both living and dying, you shall be most honored by us: and farewell; for I abhor to speak words of ill omen about the Goddess to whom your body is given as the first-fruits, the daughter of Ceres. O children, we are undone; my limbs are relaxed by grief; take me, and place me in my seat, veiling me there with these garments, O children; since neither am I pleased at these things which are done, and if the oracle were not fulfilled, life would be unbearable, for the ruin would be greater; but even this is a calamity.

CHORUS

I say that no man is either happy or miserable but through the Gods, and that the same family does not always walk in good fortune, but different fates pursue it different ways; it is wont to make one from a lofty station insignificant, and makes the wanderer wealthy: but it is impossible to avoid what is fated; no one can repel it by wisdom, but he who is hasty without purpose will always have trouble; but do not thus bear the fortune sent by the Gods, falling down in prayer, and do not over-pain your mind with grief, for she hapless possesses a glorious portion of death on behalf of her brethren and her country; nor will an inglorious reputation among men await her: but virtue proceeds through toils. These things are worthy of her father, and worthy of her noble descent; and if you respect the deaths of the good, I share your feelings.

SERVANT
O children, hail! But at what distance from this place is the aged Iolaus and your father's mother?

IOLAUS
We are here, such a presence as mine is.

SERVANT
On what account dost thou lie thus, and have an eye so downcast?

IOLAUS
A domestic care has come upon me, by which I am constrained.

SERVANT
Raise now thyself, erect thy head.

IOLAUS
I am an old man, and by no means strong.

SERVANT
But I am come, bearing to you a great joy.

IOLAUS
And who art thou, where having met you, do I forget you?

SERVANT
I am a poor servant of Hyllus; do you not recognize me, seeing me?

IOLAUS
O dearest one, dost thou then come as a savior to us from injury?

SERVANT
Surely; and moreover you are prosperous as to the present state of affairs.

IOLAUS
O mother of a doughty son, I mean Alcmena, come forth, hear these most welcome words; for you have been long wasting away as to your soul in anxiety concerning those who have come hither, where they would ever arrive.

ALCMENA
Wherefore has a mighty shout filled all this house? O Iolaus, does any herald, coming from Argos, again do you violence? my strength indeed is weak, but thus much you must know, O stranger, you shall never drag these away while I am living, else may I no longer be thought to be his mother; but if you touch them with your hand, you will have no honorable contest with two old people.

IOLAUS

Be of good cheer, old woman; fear not, the herald is not come from Argos bearing hostile words.

ALCMENA

Why then did you raise a shout, a messenger of fear?

IOLAUS

To you, that you should approach near before this temple.

ALCMENA

I do not understand this; for who is this man?

IOLAUS

He announces that your son's son is come.

ALCMENA

O! hail thou also for this news; but why and where is he now absent putting his foot in this country? what calamity prevents him from appearing hither with you, and delighting my mind?

SERVANT

He is stationing and marshaling the army which he has come bringing.

ALCMENA

I no longer understand this speech.

IOLAUS

I do; but it is my business to inquire about this.

SERVANT

What then of what has been done do you wish to learn?

IOLAUS

With how great a multitude of allies is he come?

SERVANT

With many; but I can say no other number.

IOLAUS

The chiefs of the Athenians know, I suppose.

SERVANT

They do; and they occupy the left wing.

IOLAUS

Is then the army already armed as for the work?

SERVANT

Ay; and already the victims are led away from the ranks.

IOLAUS

And how far distant is the Argive army?

SERVANT
So that the general can be distinctly seen.

IOLAUS
Doing what? arraying the ranks of the enemies?

SERVANT
We conjectured this, for we did not hear him; but I will go; I should not like my masters to join battle with the enemy, deserted as far as my part is concerned.

IOLAUS
And I will go with you; for we think the same things, being present to aid our friends as much as we can.

SERVANT
It is not your part to say a foolish word.

IOLAUS
And not to share the sturdy battle with my friends!

SERVANT
One can not see a wound from an inactive hand.

IOLAUS
But what, can not I too strike through a shield?

SERVANT
You might strike, but you yourself would fall first.

IOLAUS
No one of the enemy will dare to behold me.

SERVANT
You have not, my good friend, the strength which once you had.

IOLAUS
But I will fight with them who will not be the fewer in numbers.

SERVANT
You add but a slight weight to your friends.

IOLAUS
Do not detain me who am prepared to act.

SERVANT
You are not able to do any thing, but you may perhaps be to advise.

IOLAUS
You may say the rest, as I not staying to hear.

SERVANT
How then will you appear to the soldiers without arms?

IOLAUS
There are within this palace arms taken in war, which I will use and restore if alive; but the God will not demand them back of me, if I fall; but go in, and taking them down from the pegs, bring me as quickly as possible the panoply of a warrior; for this is a disgraceful house-keeping, for some to fight, and some to remain behind through fear.

CHORUS
Time does not depress your spirit, but it grows young again, but your body is weak: why dost thou toil in vain? which will harm you indeed, but profit our city but little; you should consider your age, and leave alone impossibilities, it can not be that you again should acquire youth.

ALCMENA
Why are you, not being in your senses, about to leave me alone with my children?

IOLAUS
For valor is the part of men; but it is your duty to take care of them.

ALCMENA
But what if you die? how shall I be saved?

IOLAUS
Your sons who are left will take care of your son.

ALCMENA
But if they, which Heaven forbid, should meet with fate!

IOLAUS
These strangers will not betray you, do not fear.

ALCMENA
Such confidence indeed I have, nothing else.

IOLAUS
And Jove, I well know, cares for your toils.

ALCMENA
Alas! Jupiter shall never be reproached by me, but he himself knows whether he is just toward me.

SERVANT
You see now this panoply of arms; but you can not make too much haste in arraying your body in them, as the contest is at hand, and, above all things, Mars hates those who delay; but if you fear the weight of arms, now then go forth unarmed, and in the ranks be clad with this equipment, and I will carry it so far.

IOLAUS
Thou hast said well; but bring the arms, having them close at hand, and put a spear in my hand, and support my left arm guiding my foot.

SERVANT
Is it right to lead a warrior like a child?

IOLAUS
One must go safely for the sake of the omen.

SERVANT
Would you were able to do as much as you are willing.

IOLAUS
Make haste, I shall suffer sadly if too late for the battle.

SERVANT
It is you who delay, and not I, seeming to do something.

IOLAUS
Do you not see how my foot presses on?

SERVANT
I see you rather seeming to hasten than hastening.

IOLAUS
You will not say so, when you behold me there.

SERVANT
Doing what? I wish I may see you successful.

IOLAUS
Striking some of the enemy through the shield.

SERVANT
If indeed we get there; for that I have fears of.

IOLAUS
Alas! O arm, would thou wert such an ally to me as I recollect you in your youth, when you ravaged Sparta with Hercules, how would I put Eurystheus to flight; since he is but a coward in abiding a spear. But in prosperity then is this too which is not right, a reputation for courage; for we think that he who is prosperous knows all things well.

CHORUS
O earth, and moon that shinest through the night, and most brilliant rays of the God, that gave light to mortals, bring me news, and shout in heaven and at the queenly throne of the blue-eyed Minerva. I am about, on behalf of my country, on behalf of my house, having received suppliants I am about to cut through danger with the white steel. It is terrible that a city, prosperous as Mycenæ, and much praised for valor in war, should nourish secret anger against my land; but it is evil too, O city, if we are to give up strangers at the bidding of Argos. Jupiter is my ally, I fear not; Jupiter rightly has favor toward me. Never shall the Gods seem inferior to men in my opinion. But, O venerable Goddess, for the soil of this land is thine, and the city of which you are mother, mistress, and guardian, lead away by some other way him who unjustly leads on this spear-brandishing host from Argos; for as far as my virtue is concerned, I do not deserve to be banished from these halls. For

honor, with much sacrifice, is ever offered to you; nor does the waning day of the month forget you, nor the songs of youths, nor the measures of dances; but on the lofty hill shouts resound in accordance with the beatings of the feet of virgins the livelong night.

SERVANT

O mistress, I bring news most concise for you to hear, and to myself most glorious; we have conquered our enemies, and trophies are set up bearing the panoply of your enemies.

ALCMENA

O best beloved, this day has caused thee to be made free for this thy news; but from one disaster you do not yet free me, for I fear whether they be living to me whom I wish to be.

SERVANT

They live, the most glorious in the army.

ALCMENA

Does not the aged Iolaus survive?

SERVANT

Surely, and having done most glorious deeds by help of the Gods.

ALCMENA

But what? has he done any doughty act in the fight?

SERVANT

He has changed from an old into a young man again.

ALCMENA

Thou tellest marvelous things, but first I wish you to relate the prosperous contest of your friends in battle.

SERVANT

One speech of mine shall tell you all this; for when stretching out our ranks face to face, we arrayed our armies against one another, Hyllus putting his foot out of his four-horse chariot, stood in the mid-space of the field; and then said, O general, you are come from Argos, why leave we not this land alone? and you will do Mycenæ no harm, depriving it of one man; but you fighting alone with me alone, either killing me, lead away the children of Hercules, or dying, allow me to possess my ancestral prerogative and palaces. And the army gave praise; that the speech was well spoken for a termination of their toils, and in respect of courage. But he neither regarding those who had heard the speech, nor, although he was general, his own character for cowardice, ventured not to come near the warlike spear, but was most cowardly; and being such, he came to enslave the descendants of Hercules. Hyllus then returned again back to his ranks; but the soothsayers, when they saw that the affair could not be arranged by single combat of one shield, sacrificed, and delayed not, but let fall forth immediately the propitious slaughter of mortal throats; and some mounted chariots, and some concealed their sides under the sides of their shields; but the king of the Athenians gave to his army such orders as become a high-born man. "O fellow-citizens, now it behooves one to defend the land that has produced and cherished us." And the other also besought his allies not to disgrace Argos and Mycenæ. But when the signal was sounded on a Tyrrhenian trumpet, and they joined battle with one another, what a clash of spears dost thou think sounded, how great a groaning and lamentation at the same time! And first the dashing on of the Argive spear broke us; then they again retreated; and next foot being interchanged with foot, and man standing against man, the battle waged fierce; and many fell; and there were two cries, O ye who dwell in Athens, O ye who sow the land of the Argives, will ye not avert disgrace from the city? And with difficulty doing every thing, not without toils did we put the Argive force to flight; and then the old man, seeing Hyllus rushing on, Iolaus, stretching forth his right hand, besought him to place him on the horse-chariot; and seizing the reins in his hands, he pressed hard upon the horses of Eurystheus.

And what happened after this I must tell by having heard from others, I myself hitherto having seen all; for passing by the venerable hill of the divine Minerva of Pellene, seeing the chariot of Eurystheus, he prayed to Juno and Jupiter to be young for one day, and to work vengeance on his enemies. But you have a marvel to hear; for two stars standing on the horse-chariot, concealed the chariot in a dim cloud, the wiser men say it was thy son and Hebe; but he from the obscure darkness showed forth a youthful image of youthful arms. And the glorious Iolaus takes the four-horse chariot of Eurystheus at the Scironian rocks—and having bound his hands in fetters, he comes bringing as glorious first-fruits of victory, the general, him who before was prosperous; but by his present fortune he proclaims clearly to all mortals to learn not to envy him who seems prosperous, till one sees him dead, as fortune is but for the day.

CHORUS

O Jupiter, thou turner to flight, now is it mine to behold a day free from dreadful fear.

ALCMENA

O Jupiter, at length you have looked upon my miseries, but still I thank you for what has been done: and I, who formerly did not think that my son dwelt with the Gods, now clearly know it. O children, now indeed you shall be free from toils, and free from Eurystheus, who shall perish miserably; and ye shall see the city of your sire, and you shall tread on your inheritance of land; and ye shall sacrifice to your ancestral gods, debarred from whom ye have had, as strangers, a wandering miserable life. But devising what clever thing has Iolaus spared Eurystheus, so as not to slay him, tell me; for in my opinion this is not wise, having taken our enemies, not to exact punishment of them.

SERVANT

Having respect for you, that with your own eyes you may see him defeated and subjected to your hand; not, indeed, of his own will, but he has bound him by force in constraint, for he was not willing to come alive into your sight and to be punished. But, O old woman, farewell, and remember for me what you first said when I began my tale. Make me free; and in such noble people as you the mouth ought to be free from falsehood.

CHORUS

To me the dance is sweet, if there be the thrilling delight of the pipe at the feast; and may Venus be kind. And sweet it is to see the good fortune of friends who did not expect it before; for the fate which accomplishes gifts gives birth to many things; and Time, the son of Saturn. You have, O city, a just path, you should never be deprived of it, to honor the Gods; and he who bids you not do so, is near madness, such proofs as these being shown. God, in truth, evidently exhorts us, taking away the arrogance of the unjust forever. Your son, O old woman, is gone to heaven; he shuns the report of having descended to the realm of Pluto, being consumed as to his body in the terrible flame of fire; and he embraces the lovely bed of Hebe in the golden hall. O Hymen, you have honored two children of Jupiter. Many things agree with many; for in truth they say that Minerva was an ally of their father, and the city and people of that Goddess has saved them, and has restrained the insolence of a man to whom passion was before justice, through violence. May my mind and soul, never be insatiable.

MESSENGER

O mistress, you see, but still it shall be said, we are come, bringing to you Eurystheus here, an unhoped-for sight, and one no less so for him to meet with, for he never expected to come into your hands when he went forth from Mycenæ with a much-toiling band of spearmen, proudly planning things much greater than his fortune, that he should destroy Athens; but the God changed his fortune, and made it contrary. Hyllus, therefore, and the good Iolaus, have set up a statue, in honor of their victory, of Jove, the putter to flight; and they send me to bring this man to you, wishing to delight your mind; for it is most delightful to see an enemy unfortunate, after having been fortunate.

ALCMENA

O hateful thing, art thou come? has justice taken you at last? first then indeed turn hither your head toward me, and dare to look your enemies in the face; for now you are ruled, and you rule no more. Art thou he, for I wish to know, who chose, O wretch, much to insult my son, though no longer existing? For in what respect didst thou not dare to insult him? who led him, while alive, down to hell, and sent him forth, bidding him destroy hydras and lions? And I am silent concerning the other evils you contrived, for it would be a long story; and it did not satisfy you that he alone should endure these things, but you drove me also, and my children, out of all Greece, sitting as suppliants of the Gods, some old, and some still infants; but you found men and a city free, who feared you not. Thou needs must die miserably, and you shall gain every thing, for you ought to die not once only, having wrought many evil deeds.

MESSENGER

It is not practicable for you to put him to death.

ALCMENA

In vain then have we taken him prisoner. But what law hinders him from dying?

MESSENGER

It seems not so to the chiefs of this land.

ALCMENA

What is this? not good to them to slay one's enemies?

MESSENGER

Not any one whom they have taken alive in battle.

ALCMENA

And did Hyllus endure this decision?

MESSENGER

He could, I suppose, disobey this land!

ALCMENA

He ought no longer to live, nor behold the light.

MESSENGER

Then first he did wrong in not dying.

ALCMENA

Then it is no longer right for him to be punished?

MESSENGER

There is no one who may put him to death.

ALCMENA
I will. And yet I say that I am some one.

MESSENGER
You will indeed have much blame if you do this.

ALCMENA
I love this city. It can not be denied. But as for this man, since he has come into my power, there is no mortal who shall take him from me. For this, whoever will may call me bold, and thinking things too much for a woman; but this deed shall be done by me.

CHORUS
It is a serious and excusable thing, O lady, for you to have hatred against this man, I well know it.

EURYSTHEUS
O woman, know plainly that I will not flatter you, nor say any thing else for my life, whence I may incur any imputation of cowardice. But not of my own accord did I undertake this strife—I knew that I was your cousin by birth, and a relation to your son Hercules; but whether I wished it or not, Juno, for it was a Goddess, forced me to toil through this ill. But when I took up enmity against him, and determined to contest this contest, I became a contriver of many evils, and sitting continually in council with myself, I brought forth many plans by night, how dispersing and slaying my enemies, I might dwell for the future not with fear, knowing that your son was not one of the many, but truly a man; for though he be mine enemy, yet shall he be well spoken of, as he was a doughty man. And when he was released from life, did it not behoove me, being hated by these children, and knowing their father's hatred to me, to move every stone, slaying and banishing them, and contriving, that, doing such things, my own affairs would have been safe? You, therefore, had you obtained my fortunes, would not have oppressed with evils the hostile offspring of a hated lion, but would wisely have permitted them to live in Argos; you will persuade no one of this. Now then, since they did not destroy me then, when I was willing, by the laws of the Greeks I shall, if slain, bear pollution to my slayer; and the city, being wise, has let me go, having greater honor for God than for its enmity toward me. And to what you said you have heard a reply: and now you may call me at once suppliant and brave. Thus is the case with me, I do not wish to die, but I should not be grieved at leaving life.

CHORUS
I wish, O Alcmena, to advise you a little, to let go this man, since it seems so to the city.

ALCMENA
But how, if he both die, and still we obey the city?

CHORUS
That would be best; but how can that be?

ALCMENA
I will teach you, easily; for having slain him, then I will give his corpse to those of his friends who come after him; for I will not deny his body to the earth, but he dying, shall satisfy my revenge.

EURYSTHEUS

Slay me, I do not deprecate thy wrath. But this city indeed, since it has released me, and feared to slay me, I will present with an ancient oracle of Apollo, which, in time, will be of greater profit than you would expect; for ye will bury me when I am dead, where it is fated, before the temple of the divine virgin of Pallene; and being well disposed to you, and a protector to the city, I shall ever lie as a sojourner under the ground, but most hostile to their descendants when they come hither with much force, betraying this kindness: such strangers do ye now defend. How then did I, knowing this, come hither, and not respect the oracle of the God? Thinking Juno far more powerful than oracles, and that she would not betray me, I did so. But suffer neither libations nor blood to be poured on my tomb, for I will give them an evil return as a requital for these things; and ye shall have a double gain from me, I will both profit you and injure them by dying.

ALCMENA

Why then do ye delay, if you are fated to accomplish safety to the city and to your descendants, to slay this man, hearing these things? for they show us the safest path. The man is an enemy, but he will profit us dying. Take him away, O servants; then having slain him, ye must give him to the dogs; for hope not thou, that living, thou shalt again banish me from my native land.

CHORUS

These things seem good to me, proceed, O attendants, for every thing on our part shall be done completely for our sovereigns.

Euripides – A Short Biography

Euripides is rightly lauded as one of the great dramatists of all time. In his lifetime, he wrote over 90 plays and although only 18 have survived they reveal the scope and reach of his genius.

Euripides is identified with many theatrical innovations that have influenced drama all the way down to modern times, especially in the representation of traditional, mythical heroes as ordinary people in extraordinary circumstances. This new approach led him to pioneer developments that later writers would adapt to comedy. Yet he also became "the most tragic of poets", focusing on the inner lives and motives of his characters in a way previously unknown. He was "the creator of...that cage which is the theatre of Shakespeare's Othello, Racine's Phèdre, of Ibsen and Strindberg," in which "...imprisoned men and women destroy each other by the intensity of their loves and hates", and yet he was also the literary ancestor of comic dramatists as diverse as Menander and George Bernard Shaw.

As would be expected from a life lived 2,500 years ago, details of it are few and far between. Accounts of his life, written down the ages, do exist but whether much is reliable or surmised is open to debate.

Most accounts agree that he was born on Salamis Island around 480 BC, to mother Cleito and father Mnesarchus, a retailer who lived in a village near Athens. Upon the receipt of an oracle saying that his son was fated to win "crowns of victory", Mnesarchus insisted that the boy should train for a career in athletics.

His education was not only confined to athletics: he also studied painting and philosophy under the masters Prodicus and Anaxagoras.

However, what became quickly very clear was that athletics was not to be his way to win crowns of victory. Euripides had been lucky enough to have been born in the era as the other two masters of Greek Tragedy; Sophocles and Æschylus. It was in their footsteps that he was destined to follow.

His first play was performed some thirteen years after the first of Socrates plays and a mere three years after Æschylus had written his classic The Oristria.

Theatre was becoming a very important part of the Greek culture. The Dionysia, held annually, was the most important festival of theatre and second only to the fore-runner of the Olympic games, the Panathenia, held every four years, in its appeal. It was a large festival in ancient Athens in honor of the god Dionysus, the central events of which were the theatrical performances of dramatic tragedies and, from 487 BC, comedies. The Dionysia actually consisted of two related festivals, the Rural Dionysia and the City Dionysia, which took place in different parts of the year.

Euripides first competed in the City Dionysia, in 455 BC, one year after the death of Æschylus, and, incredibly, it was not until 441 BC that he won first prize. His final competition in Athens was in 408 BC. However, The Bacchae and Iphigenia in Aulis were performed after his death in 405 BC and first prize was awarded posthumously. Altogether his plays won first prize only five times.

His plays, and those of Æschylus and Sophocles, indicate a difference in outlook between the three men, most easily explained as a generational gap, although with three great talents overlapping the driving forces may have pushed individual styles onwards perhaps faster than they may otherwise have done. Æschylus still looked back to the archaic period, Sophocles was in transition between periods, and Euripides was fully bonded with the new spirit of the classical age. When Euripides' plays are sequenced in time, they also show a developing pattern:

An early period of high tragedy (Medea, Hippolytus)
A patriotic period at the outset of the Peloponnesian War (Children of Hercules, Suppliants)
A middle period of disillusionment at the senselessness of war (Hecuba, Women of Troy)
An escapist period with a focus on romantic intrigue (Ion, Iphigenia in Tauris, Helen)
A final period of tragic despair (Orestes, Phoenician Women, Bacchae)

However, with over three quarters of his plays lost it is difficult to be certain as to whether the other works would also represent this development (e.g., Iphigenia at Aulis is dated with the 'despairing' Bacchae, yet it contains elements that became typical of New Comedy). In the Bacchae, he restores the chorus and messenger speech to their traditional role in the tragic plot, and the play appears to be the culmination of a regressive or archaizing tendency in his later works.

In one of his earliest surviving plays, Medea, includes a speech that he seems to have written in defence of himself as an intellectual ahead of his time, and to further challenge the times he has put the words in the mouth of the play's heroine:

"If you introduce new, intelligent ideas to fools, you will be thought frivolous, not intelligent. On the other hand, if you do get a reputation for surpassing those who are supposed to be intellectually sophisticated, you will seem to be a thorn in the city's flesh. This is what has happened to me." — Medea.

As we know Athenian tragedies during Euripides' lifetime were a public contest between playwrights. The state funded that contest and awarded prizes to the winners. The language was spoken and sung verse, the performance area included a circular floor or orchestra where the chorus could dance, a space for actors (usually three speaking actors in Euripides' time), a backdrop or skene and some special effects: an ekkyklema (used to bring the skene's "indoors" outdoors) and a mechane (used to lift actors in the air, as in deus ex machina). With the introduction of the third actor (an innovation attributed to Sophocles), acting also began to be regarded as a skill to be rewarded with prizes, requiring a long apprenticeship in the chorus. Euripides and other playwrights accordingly composed more and more arias for accomplished actors to sing and this tendency becomes more marked in his later plays: tragedy for him was a living and ever-changing genre.

Accounts by the famed comic poet, Aristophanes, characterise Euripides as a spokesman for destructive, new ideas, that mirror or help to bring about declining standards in both society and tragedy. However, 5th century tragedy was a social gathering for "carrying out quite publicly the maintenance and development of mental infrastructure" and it offered spectators a "platform for an utterly unique form of institutionalized discussion". A dramatist's role was not just to entertain but also to educate his fellow citizens—he was expected to have a message. Clearly this use of drama to democratize discussion was a very useful tool for all sides. Traditional myth provided the subject matter but the dramatist was meant to be innovative so as to sustain interest, which led to novel characterization of heroic figures and to use the mythical past to talk about present issues. The difference between Euripides and his older colleagues was, again, one of degree: his characters talked about the present more controversially and more pointedly than did those of Æschylus and Sophocles, sometimes even challenging the democratic order. Thus, for example, Odysseus is represented in Hecuba as "agile-minded, sweet-talking, demos-pleasing" i.e., a type of the war-time demagogues that were active in Athens during the Peloponnesian War. His concept is pleasingly simple. He retains the old stories and myths as well as the great names of the past and places them in the lives of contemporary Athenians thereby immediately help the audience understand it from the point of view of their own lives.

As mouthpieces for contemporary issues, they all seem to have had at least an elementary course in public speaking. Sometimes the dialogue often contrasts so strongly with the mythical and heroic setting, it looks as if Euripides aimed at parody, as for example in The Trojan Women, where the heroine's rationalized prayer provokes comment from Menelaus:

Hecuba:...O Zeus, whether you are the Law of Necessity in nature, or the Law of Reason in man, hear my prayers. You are everywhere, pursuing your noiseless path, ordering the affairs of mortals according to justice.

Menelaus: What's this? You are starting a new fashion in prayer.

Athenian citizens were familiar with rhetoric in the assembly and law courts, and some scholars believe that Euripides was more interested in his characters as speakers with cases to argue than as characters with lifelike personalities. They are self-conscious about speaking formally and their rhetoric is shown to be flawed, as if Euripides was exploring the problematical nature of language and communication: "For speech points in three different directions at once, to the speaker, to the person addressed, to the features in the world it describes, and each of these directions can be felt as skewed". Thus in the example above, Hecuba presents herself as a sophisticated intellectual describing a rationalised cosmos yet the speech is ill-matched to her audience, Menelaus (an unsophisticated listener), and soon it is found not to suit the cosmos either (her infant grandson is brutally murdered by the victorious Greeks).

Æschylus and Sophocles were innovative, but Euripides could move easily between tragic, comic, romantic and political effects, a versatility that appears in individual plays and also over the course of his career. Potential for comedy lay in his use of 'contemporary' characters, in his sophisticated tone, his relatively informal Greek, and his ingenious use of plots centered on motifs that later became standard, such as the 'recognition scene'. Other tragedians also used recognition scenes but they were heroic in emphasis, as in Æschylus's The Libation Bearers, which Euripides parodied with his mundane treatment of it in Electra (Euripides was unique among the tragedians in incorporating theatrical criticism in his plays). Traditional myth, with its exotic settings, heroic adventures and epic battles, offered potential for romantic melodrama as well as for political comments on a war theme, so that his plays are an extraordinary mix of elements. The Trojan Women for example is a powerfully disturbing play on the theme of war's horrors, apparently critical of Athenian imperialism (it was composed in the aftermath of the Melian massacre and during the preparations for the Sicilian Expedition) yet it features the comic exchange between Menelaus and Hecuba quoted above and the chorus considers Athens, the "blessed land of Theus", to be a desirable refuge—such complexity and ambiguity are typical both of his "patriotic" and "anti-war" plays.

Tragic poets in the 5th century competed against one another at the City Dionysia, each with a tetralogy consisting of three tragedies and a satyr-play. The few extant fragments of satyr-plays attributed to Æschylus and Sophocles indicate that these were a loosely structured, simple and jovial form of entertainment. However, in Cyclops (the only complete Euripides satyr-play that survives) the entertainment is structured more like a tragedy and introduced a note of critical irony typical of his other work. His genre-bending inventiveness is shown above all in Alcestis, a blend of tragic and satyric elements. This fourth play in his tetralogy for 438 BC (i.e., it occupied the position conventionally reserved for satyr-plays) is a "tragedy" that features Heracles as a satyric hero in conventional satyr-play scenes, involving an arrival, a banquet, a victory over an ogre (in this case, Death), a happy ending, a feast and a departure to new adventures.

Euripides was also a great lyric poet. In Medea, for example, he composed for his city, Athens, "the noblest of her songs of praise". His lyric skills however are not just confined to individual poems: "A play of Euripides is a musical whole....one song echoes motifs from the preceding song, while introducing new ones."

Much of his life and his whole career coincided with the struggle between Athens and Sparta for hegemony in Greece but he didn't live to see the final defeat of his city.

It is said that he died in Macedonia after being attacked by the Molossian hounds of King Archelaus and that his cenotaph near Piraeus was struck by lightning—signs of his unique powers, whether for good or ill. In an account by Plutarch, the complete failure of the Sicilian expedition led Athenians to trade renditions of Euripides' lyrics to their enemies in return for food and drink (Life of Nicias 29). Plutarch is the source also for the story that the victorious Spartan generals, having planned the demolition of Athens and the enslavement of its people, grew merciful after being entertained at a banquet by lyrics from Euripides' play Electra: "they felt that it would be a barbarous act to annihilate a city which produced such men" (Life of Lysander).

In The Frogs, composed after Euripides and Æschylus were both dead, Aristophanes imagines the god Dionysus venturing down to Hades in search of a good poet to bring back to Athens. After a debate between the two deceased bards, the god brings Æschylus back to life as more useful to Athens on account of his wisdom, rejecting Euripides as merely clever. Such comic 'evidence' suggests that Athenians admired Euripides even while they mistrusted his intellectualism, at least during the long war with Sparta.

Euripides had a famous library—one of the first to be privately collected. Although he lived most of his life in the midst of the cultured society of Athens, and was in some respects a leader in it, he grew bitter and despondent over the fierce rivalries and greedy ambitions which ran through the city. He loved the seclusion of his house at Salamis, where it was said that he composed his dramas in a cave.

Euripides fell out of favour with his fellow Athenian citizens and retired to the court of Archelaus, king of Macedon, who treated him with consideration and affection.

At his death, in around 406BC, he was mourned by the king, who, refusing the request of the Athenians that his remains be carried back to the Greek city, buried him with much splendor within his own dominions. His tomb was placed at the confluence of two streams, near Arethusa in Macedonia, and a cenotaph was built to his memory on the road from Athens towards the Piraeus.

Euripides – A Concise Bibliography

Alcestis (438 BC)
Medea (431 BC)
Heracleidae (c. 430 BC)
Hippolytus (428 BC)
Andromache (c. 425 BC)
Hecuba (c. 424 BC)
The Suppliants (c. 423 BC)
Electra (c. 420 BC)
Heracles (c. 416 BC)
The Trojan Women (c. 415 BC)
Iphigenia in Tauris (c. 414 BC)
Ion (c. 414 BC)
Helen (c. 412 BC)
Phoenician Women (c. 410 BC)
Orestes (c.408 BC)
Bacchae (405 BC)
Iphigenia at Aulis (405 BC)
Rhesus
Cyclops

Lost and Fragmentary Plays (Dated)

Peliades (455 BC)
Telephus (438 BC with Alcestis)
Alcmaeon in Psophis (438 BC with Alcestis)
Cretan Women (438 with Alcestis)
Cretans (c. 435 BC)
Philoctetes (431 BC with Medea)
Dictys (431 BC with Medea)
Theristai (satyr play, 431 BC with Medea)
Stheneboea (before 429 BC)
Bellerophon (c. 430 BC)
Cresphontes (ca. 425 BC)
Erechtheus (422 BC)
Phaethon (c. 420 BC)

Wise Melanippe (c. 420 BC)
Alexandros (415 BC with Trojan Women)
Palamedes (415 BC with Trojan Women)
Sisyphus (satyr play, 415 BC with Trojan Women)
Captive Melanippe (c. 412 BC)
Andromeda (412 BC with Helen)
Antiope (c. 410 BC)
Archelaus (c. 410 BC)
Hypsipyle (c. 410 BC)
Alcmaeon in Corinth (c. 405 BC) Won first prize as part of a trilogy with The Bacchae and Iphigenia in Aulis.

Lost and Fragmentary Plays (Not Dated)

Aegeus
Aeolus
Alcmene
Alope, or Cercyon
Antigone
Auge
Autolycus
Busiris
Cadmus
Chrysippus
Danae
Epeius
Eurystheus
Hippolytus Veiled
Ino
Ixion
Lamia
Licymnius
Meleager
Mysians
Oedipus
Oeneus
Oenomaus
Peirithous
Peleus
Phoenix
Phrixus
Pleisthenes
Polyidus
Protesilaus
Reapers
Rhadamanthys
Sciron
Scyrians
Syleus
Temenidae